Musical Forms
Listening Scores

Roy Bennett

Listening Scores provides a collection of musical scores of different kinds selected from composers from the 17th to 20th centuries. A development of and extension to the material dealt with in *Musical Forms* Books 1–3, it covers the various musical forms, structures and types of composition.

Listening Scores is essentially a listening activity book backed up by a cassette which includes many of the pieces described in the book. Basic concepts and perceptions important to the listening element of GCSE syllabuses are covered, e.g. instrumentation, voices, rhythm and meter, key and tonality, cadences, accompaniment, mood and character, tension and resolution, various melodic and rhythmic devices, texture, timbre, contrast, Italian terms.

An understanding of the various musical forms and structures illustrated will be useful to pupils preparing for GCSE when composing their own pieces and may also encourage them to experiment with new structures of their own devising.

Contents

Binary form — 3
Handel: Piece No. 18 from the 'Water Music' — 3
Handel: *Bourrée* from the 'Royal Fireworks Music' — 3
Bach: *Sarabande* and *Gavotte* from 'French' Suite No. 6 — 4

Ternary form — 5
Schumann: Piece No. 4 from *Papillons* — 5
Prokofiev: *Masks* from 'Romeo and Juliet' — 6
Prokofiev: *Montagues and Capulets* from 'Romeo and Juliet' — 6
Tchaikovsky: *Andante cantabile* from String Quartet No. 1 — 7
Verdi: *Celeste Aida* from the opera 'Aida' — 10, 11

Simple rondo form — 12
Mozart: *Rondo* from Horn Concerto No. 2 in Eb major (K417) — 12

Project 1 — 18
Purcell: Hornpipe in E minor — 18
Khatchaturian: *Dance of the Rose Maidens* from 'Gayaneh' — 18
Khatchaturian: *Sabre Dance* from 'Gayaneh' — 19
Bach: *Forlane* from Orchestral Suite No. 1 — 20
Mozart: *Lacrymosa* from Requiem in D minor — 20

Ritornello form — 23
Vivaldi: First movement of the Concerto 'Autumn' from *The Four Seasons* — 23

Minuet and Trio form — 25
Mozart: *Minuet* from Symphony No. 36 in C major (The 'Linz') — 25, 26
Scherzo and Trio — 28
Beethoven: *Scherzo* from Piano Sonata No. 2 in A major, Opus 2 No. 2 — 28

Variation form (theme and variations) — 29
Bizet: *Prélude* to 'L'Arlésienne' — 29
Mozart: Variations on *Unser dummer Pöbel* (K455) — 30
Beethoven: Fourth movement from Septet in E flat — 32

The Ground Bass — 34
Purcell: 'Sound the Trumpet' — 34
Brahms: *Finale* from 'Variations on a Theme by Haydn' — 36

Project 2 — 38
Mozart: Third movement from Clarinet Quintet in A major (K581) — 38
Beethoven: *Scherzo* from Symphony No. 2 in D major — 39
Delius: *Brigg Fair* (excerpt) — 40
Copland: Variations on a Shaker song, from the ballet 'Appalachian Spring' — 41
Walton: *The Death of Falstaff* from music for the film 'Henry V' — 41

Da capo aria — 42
Handel: *Dove sei* ('Art thou troubled') from 'Rodelinda' — 42

Lieder: strophic and through-composed — 44
Schumann: Song No. 1 from *Dichterliebe* — 44
Schubert: *Erlkönig* (The Erlking) — 46

Project 3 — 48
Schubert: *Der Tod und das Mädchen* (Death and the Maiden) — 48

Canon and Fugue — 49
Canon — 49
Bizet: *Farandole* from 'L'Arlésienne' Suite 2 — 49
Bach: Chorale prelude: *In dulci jubilo* — 49, 50
Fugue — 51
Bach: Fugue in C minor from 'The Well-tempered Clavier', Book 2 — 52
Handel: First two movements from Concerto Grosso in G minor, Opus 6 No. 6 — 53

Project 4 — 56
Handel: Recitative *All they that see Him*, and Chorus *He trusted in God*, from 'Messiah' — 56, 57

Sonata Form — 62
Mendelssohn: Overture – *The Hebrides* (*Fingal's Cave*) — 63

Abridged sonata form — 66
Rossini: Overture to *La Gazza Ladra* (The Thievish Magpie) — 67

Sonata-rondo form — 71
Beethoven: Third movement from Violin Concerto in D major — 72

Project 5
Bach: Chorale – *Jesu, Joy of Man's Desiring* — 76
Handel: Coronation Anthem – *Zadok the Priest* — 76, 77
Delius: *On Hearing the First Cuckoo in Spring* — 79, 80

Binary form

A piece of music which is designed in *binary form* is built up in *two* sections of music: **A** and **B**. Section **A** makes a musical statement which sounds incomplete on its own. This is answered, and balanced, by the music of section **B**. Usually, both sections are marked to be repeated.

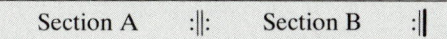

In most pieces in binary form, the music modulates towards the end of section **A** so that this section ends in a new key. If the tonic key is a major key, then usually this modulation is to the dominant key. If the tonic is a minor key, the modulation will very likely be to the relative major (the major key which shares the same key signature). During section **B**, the music returns to the tonic key.

In a binary piece both sections, **A** and **B**, usually share the same musical ideas. The tune which begins section **A** is likely to be repeated at the beginning of section **B** – but in a new key, and, for more interest, perhaps presented in a different way. For example:
  in *inversion*: the tune is 'turned upside down' – intervals originally rising, now fall (and vice versa);
  or put down into the bass;
  or used to build a *sequence* (in which a tuneful phrase is immediately repeated at a slightly higher or lower pitch).

In some binary pieces the two sections, **A** and **B**, are equal in length. In many others, however, section **B** is longer than section **A**, and the composer may take the music of **B** through several related keys before making 'for home' and closing in the tonic key:

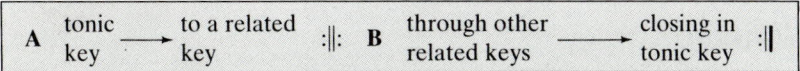

Section **A** may end with a distinctive musical idea which reappears at the end of the section **B** – so that the endings of the two sections are alike, except for key.

Piece No. 18 from the 'Water Music' — Handel (1685–1759)

Handel's 'Water Music', first performed in 1717 during a royal procession on the River Thames, consists of 20 pieces. Listen to this short binary piece, which is in the style of a gigue. It is for two piccolos or small recorders, strings (without double basses), and continuo.

Follow-up

1. How many bars long is each section, **A** and **B**, in this binary piece?
2. In which key is this music? In which key does section **A** end?
3. **B** begins with the same tune as **A**. How is it presented?

   | in inversion | as a sequence | or | put down into the bass |

4. Suggest a word (or words) to describe the mood of this piece.

Bourrée from the 'Royal Fireworks Music' — Handel

This dance is from Handel's suite which he composed in 1749 for the royal firework display in Green Park, London. In the recording on the cassette, this Bourrée is played with repeats; then it is played through again, without repeats. So the pattern you will *hear* is A A B B A B. But the repeats in no way alter the basic structure of the piece, which is in binary form – in two sections, **AB**.

Follow-up

1. In which key is this Bourrée?
2. In which key does **A** end and **B** begin?
3. Which instruments play **A** and **B** each time they are heard?
4. Handel's 'Royal Fireworks Music' is a suite. What is a suite?

Sarabande and Gavotte*
from 'French' Suite
No. 6 in E major
Bach (1685–1750)

These two contrasting dances are from the last of a set of six keyboard suites which Bach composed around 1715. The sixth 'French' Suite includes eight dances altogether: allemande, courante, sarabande, gavotte, polonaise, bourrée, menuet, and gigue. Bach structures all eight dances in binary form.

Sarabande

Follow-up

1. How many bars is each section, **A** and **B**, in this piece?
2. **B** begins with the same tune as **A**. Is the tune:
   - i) presented in inversion?
   - ii) put down into the bass?
   - iii) used to build up a sequence?
   - iv) merely transposed into a new key?
3. Name some of the ornaments which Bach uses to decorate this music.
4. Suggest a word (or words) to describe the mood of this Sarabande.
5. (a) On which instrument is this music played?
   (b) What is the main difference between the way sounds are produced on this instrument, and the way they are produced on a harpsichord?

Gavotte

Follow-up

1. How many beats to a bar has this Gavotte?
2. Suggest an Italian term to match the speed of this music.
3. Section **B** begins with the same tune as section **A**. In which of the following ways is it presented?

   | in inversion | as a sequence | put down into the bass |

4. In what way is the ending of section **B** similar to the ending of section **A** – and in what ways is it different?
5. In what ways does the Gavotte contrast, in mood and character, with the Sarabande?
6. Which of the movements in Bach's 'French' Suite No. 6 are the four 'standard' movements of the Baroque keyboard suite, and which are *galanterien* (optional extra movements)?

[* In the performance of these dances on the cassette, repeats are not observed.]

Ternary form

A piece designed in *ternary form* is built up in *three* sections of music: **A B A** – making a 'musical sandwich'. **A¹** and **A²** use the same music.

Music **B**, the 'filling' in the sandwich, presents some kind of contrast to music **A**, and is called an **episode**:

A¹	B	A²
	(an episode)	
statement	contrast	restatement

There are many ways in which a composer may achieve musical contrast (or *difference*) between music **A** and music **B**. Most effective of all is for music **B** to introduce a completely different tune. Also important, in most pieces, is the contrast of different, but 'related' keys; and this often involves a contrast of mode (major/minor). Other possible contrasts include changes of mood, speed, rhythm, time or metre (the number of beats to a bar), dynamics (soft/loud), pitch (high/low), contrasts of musical textual (dense/thin, heavy/light, *legato*/*staccato*, and so on) and contrasts of timbre (tone-colour).

When music **A** returns as **A²** in the third section of the piece, it may be exactly the same as at first – or the composer may provide more interest by making changes of some kind. If **A²** is an *exact* repetition of **A¹**, the composer may not trouble to write out the music of **A** again. In this case, at the end of music **B** will be printed the Italian phrase *da capo* (or simply *D.C.*) meaning 'repeat from the beginning', and the word *fine* ('end') will be printed at the end of music **A**.

A ternary piece may begin with a short introduction, and the music may be rounded off with a **coda** (Italian for 'tail'). A short passage of music called a **link** may join one section smoothly to the next.

Piece No. 4 from *Papillons* Schumann (1810–1856)

Papillons (Butterflies) is a set of twelve short, dance-like piano pieces which Schumann composed between 1829 and 1831. The fourth piece, in the key of F♯ minor, is designed in ternary form.

Before listening

Look at the music of this ternary piece and notice where each section begins. Schumann marks the music of **A¹** to be repeated, and so the plan of this piece is ‖: **A¹** :‖ **B A²** ‖.

Follow-up

1. Mention some of ways in which music **B** presents a contrast to music **A** in this ternary piece.
2. When music **A** returns as **A²**, is it exactly the same as at first – or does Schumann change it in any way?

Masks from 'Romeo and Juliet'

Prokofiev (1891–1953)

Prokofiev based his ballet 'Romeo and Juliet' on Shakespeare's play. *Masks* is danced, with youthful exuberance, by Romeo, Mercutio and Benvolio as they arrive, uninvited, at the Capulets' ball. They wear masks to disguise the fact that they belong to the Montague family.

Follow-up

1. At which bar does section **B** begin in this ternary piece?
2. At which bar does music **A** return as **A²**?
3. Listen to *Masks* again and note down any musical contrasts (differences) you hear between music **B** and music **A**.

Montagues and Capulets from 'Romeo and Juliet'

Prokofiev

This is the first piece in the Second Suite which Prokofiev arranged from his ballet. He structures the music in ternary form, with a short, powerfully dramatic introduction.

As you listen

A¹ (aggressively rhythmic, suggesting the arrogant swagger of the Montagues and Capulets), is quite lengthy. But you will find it easy to tell where the contrasting section **B** begins, and where music **A** returns as **A²**.

Follow-up

1. The introduction to the piece is intensely dramatic. How does Prokofiev build up tension in the music here? How is this tension resolved or relaxed?
2. In a ternary piece it is important that there should be musical contrasts (differences) between music **A** and music **B**. In this piece, the main contrast is a sudden change of *mood* – and also of *timbre* (instrumental tone-colours). Describe the mood of music **B**. Identify some of the special timbres in this section of the piece.
3. What difference is there in musical *texture* between **A** and **B**?
4. Note down any other contrasts you hear between **A** and **B**.
5. When music **A** returns as **A²**, is it exactly the same as at first – or does Prokofiev make any important changes?

Andante cantabile Tchaikovsky (1840–1893)

This is a movement from Tchaikovsky's First String Quartet (composed in 1872) but it is often played by a string orchestra. The opening melody is a Russian folksong that Tchaikovsky heard one day sung by a carpenter working outside his room. The music is in ternary form.

As you listen

See if you can tell where section **B** begins, and where music **A** returns as **A²**.

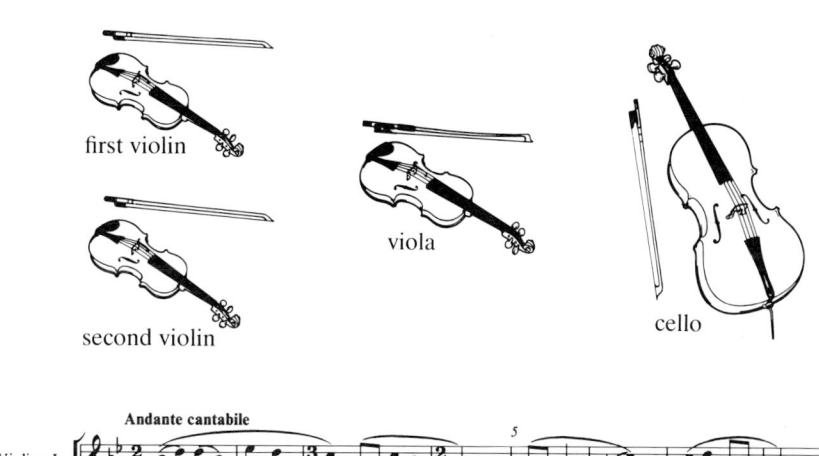

Follow-up

1. Describe the mood at the beginning of this piece. What qualities in the music, and the instrumental sound, especially help to conjure up this mood?
2. In this ternary piece, does section **B** immediately follow **A¹**, or does Tchaikovsky join these sections smoothly together with a link?
3. In which bars of this piece is an *ostinato* played?
4. The **coda** is quite lengthy. Is it built from entirely new musical ideas – or do you hear any ideas from earlier on in the movement?

Celeste Aida from 'Aida'   Verdi (1813–1901)

Verdi's opera 'Aida', the story of which takes place in ancient Egypt, was first performed in Cairo in 1871. The hero, Radamès, sings the recitative *Se quel guerrier io fossi!* followed by the famous aria *Celeste Aida* soon after the beginning of Act I.

Recitative If only I were that warrior!
If my dreams were to come true!
An army of heroes, with me as their leader —
then victory, and the praise of all Memphis!
To come back to you, my sweet Aida,
wearing the victor's laurel wreath, saying:
'For you I fought, for you I vanquished!'

Aria Heavenly Aida, divine form,
mystical garland of light and flowers,
of all my thoughts you are the queen,
you are the splendour of my whole life.
If I could only give back to you the blue skies,
the gentle breezes, of your native land;
offer you a royal wreath to deck your hair,
raise a royal throne for you, in the sun!
Heavenly Aida, divine form,
mystical radiance of light and flowers, (*etc.*)

Before listening

Find out about the story of Verdi's opera 'Aida'.

After listening

Discover answers to these questions, listening again to the music if necessary:
1. Which type of voice sings this music?
2. How does Verdi, in the opening recitative, vary the accompaniment to match the meaning of the words?
3. Verdi structures the aria in ternary form, **A¹ B A²**, rounded off with a coda. At which bar does **B** begin? At which bar does music **A** return as **A²**? Where does the coda begin?
4. Describe the music of the coda. (Verdi adds some extraordinary dynamic markings. In the performance you are listening to, does the singer obey all these markings?)
5. Verdi's opera 'Aida' is of the type often described as a *grand opera*. What ingredients (musical and theatrical) would you expect to find in a *grand opera*?

Recitativo

Radamès: Se quel guerrier io fossi! se il mio sogna si averasse!

Allegro vivo *con entusiasmo*

Un esercito di prodi da me guidato e la vittoria e il plauso di Menfi tutta! E a te, mia dolce Aida, tornar di lauri cinto dirti: per te ho pugnato, per te ho vinto!

Andantino *con espress.*

dolce

Celeste Aida, forma divina, mistico serto di luce e fior, del mio pensiero tu sei regina, tu di mia vita sei lo splendor. Il tuo bel cielo vorrei ridarti, le dolci brezze del patrio suol: un regal serto sul crin posarti, ergerti un trono vicino al sol, ah!

Celeste Aida, forma divina, mistico raggio di luce e fior, del mio pensiero tu sei regina, tu di mia vita sei lo splendor.

parlante ppp

Il tuo bel cielo vorrei ridarti, le dolci brezze del patrio suol; un regal serto sul crin posarti, ergerti un trono vicino al sol, un trono vicino al sol, un trono vicino al sol.

allarg. e morendo

Simple rondo form

In a piece designed in simple rondo form, the main theme (**A**) keeps 'coming round', with contrasting sections of music called *episodes* heard in between. Below is a plan for a simple rondo with two episodes. (Some rondos have three or more episodes, and so the main theme then comes round four or more times.)

The rondo theme (**A**) is always in the tonic key, while each of the episodes visits a related key. A *link* may join sections smoothly together. Each time the rondo theme returns it may be shortened or somehow varied, and its final appearance may be followed by a *coda*.

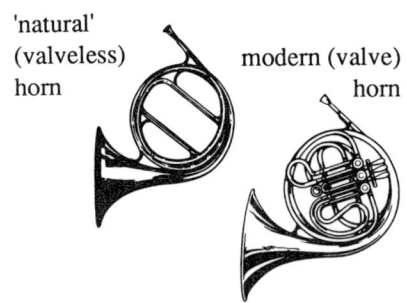

Rondo from Horn Concerto No. 2 in E flat (K417) Mozart (1756–1791)

Mozart wrote his four Horn Concertos for a talented player named Leutgeb who kept a cheese-shop in Vienna. Mozart enjoyed a joke, and the manuscripts of the concertos are covered with joking remarks directed against Leutgeb. This second concerto has the dedication: 'Wolfgang Amadé Mozart has taken pity on Leutgeb, ass, ox and fool, Vienna 27th May 1783'. Other remarks are scattered throughout the score. Even so, composer and player were in fact the best of friends!

Before listening

Look through the score of this rondo, which is given in full. On the opening page there are two *systems* of score. All the remaining pages carry three systems, separated by pairs of slanting lines (//). In following the score, you will find that the melodic interest is either in the solo horn part (*Corno principale*, or *Cor. pr.*) or the first violins' stave, immediately below the solo horn part.

After listening

1. (a) How many times does the main rondo theme appear?
   (b) How many episodes are there in this rondo?
2. When the rondo theme returns for the last time, how does Mozart bring touches of humour into the music?
3. Which of the episodes do you think presents most contrast to the rondo theme? In what ways?

Project 1

In each of the next five pieces, the composer structures the music in either binary form, ternary form, or simple rondo form. Listen to each piece (as many times as necessary) following the score.

(a) As you listen, decide which form the composer is using to structure the music.
(b) Afterwards: draw a diagram, or make out a plan, showing how the music is built up.
(c) Mention any interesting points about the music. For example: interesting instrumentation; how the music of a new section introduces striking contrasts; whether a main musical idea, when it reappears later, is changed in some way – or is the same as when it was first heard; any other points of interest.

1. Hornpipe in E minor — Purcell (1659–1695)

2. Dance of the Rose Maidens — Khatchaturian (1903–1978)

Both this piece and the next are dances from Khatchaturian's vividly orchestrated ballet 'Gayaneh'.

3. Sabre Dance
Khatchaturian

4. *Forlane* from *Orchestral Suite No. 1*   Bach (1685–1750)

Bach composed the first of his four Orchestral Suites at some time between 1717 and 1721. The music is scored for 2 oboes and 1 bassoon, strings, and continuo. The suite is in seven movements, of which this Forlane is the fourth. Originally a forlane (or furlano) was a lively Italian folkdance; by Bach's time it had become an aristocratic French court dance, rather similar to the gigue.

5. *Lacrymosa* from *Requiem in D minor*   Mozart (1756–1791)

The Requiem was Mozart's last work. He had received a visit from a mysterious stranger, dressed all in grey, who had commissioned him to compose a requiem – but 'in secret'. (It is now believed that the stranger was a messenger from a wealthy count who intended to pass off the composition as his own.) Mozart set to work; but the Requiem remained unfinished at his death and was completed by his pupil, Süssmayer. The music of the *Lacrymosa* (No. 7 of the twelve movements) was composed by Mozart, but orchestrated by Süssmayer.

> Tearful that day when, from the dust, guilty man shall arise to be judged. Spare him therefore, O God. Blessèd Jesu, O Lord, grant them rest. Amen.

Ritornello form

This is the name given to the form or structure often used to build up the quicker movements (and sometimes also the slower movements) in a Baroque concerto grosso or solo concerto.

The Italian word **ritornello** means a 'little return'. In ritornello form, the main theme – the ritornello itself – is introduced by the ripieno group, usually with the soloist(s) joining in, and it then returns at other points throughout the movement. It may reappear in full or it may be shortened or varied. Its first and last appearances are in the tonic key; at other times it is generally in another key.

Appearances of the ritornello are separated by **episodes** which feature the soloist (or solo group). An episode may introduce new musical ideas, or it may be based on one or more ideas taken from the ritornello. And so a plan of the music may be shown as:

Tutti 1 (Ritornello)	Solo 1 (Episode)	Tutti 2 (Ritornello)	Solo 2 (Episode)	Tutti 3 (Ritornello)	and so on . . .

Baroque composers sometimes used this same structure in other types of music – for example, to build up an aria or a chorus in a work such as an opera, a cantata, or an oratorio.

First movement from Violin Concerto in F major, Opus 8 No. 3, 'Autumn' from *The Four Seasons* Vivaldi (1678–1741)

The Four Seasons consists of four solo concertos for violin, string orchestra (*ripieno* group) and *continuo* (harpsichord and cello). These concertos are programmatic – or descriptive – works, based on poems (possibly by Vivaldi himself) describing the different seasons of the year. Vivaldi breaks up each poem into sections and prints these throughout the score, indicating those points where his music vividly illustrates the ideas mentioned in the poem.

The third concerto, 'Autumn', is in three contrasting movements (quick : slow : quick). The first and last are in ritornello form. In this first movement, peasants celebrate the gathering in of a rich and fruitful harvest with dance and song – and also a considerable amount of wine!

As you listen

Spot each return of the *ritornello*. Also, notice where quotations from the poem occur – and how Vivaldi illustrates these in his music.

Follow-up

1. How many times does the ritornello appear during this movement?
2. How many episodes are there?
3. Draw a diagram, beginning like the one below showing how Vivaldi plans and builds up the music of the complete movement.

Tutti 1	Solo 1	Tutti 2	
Ritornello (bar 1)	Episode (bar 14)	Ritornello (bar 27)	(and so on . . .)

4. (a) At the beginning of the first episode, does the solo violinist bring in an entirely new idea, or is the material taken from the ritornello?
   (b) Which instruments accompany the solo violin during this first episode? What name is given to the part played by these instruments in a Baroque composition of this kind?
   (c) For most of the time during this first episode the soloist plays double-stoppings. What are 'double-stoppings'?
5. At which bars, during the second episode, does Vivaldi write a sequence?
6. Listen to the movement again. On each occasion when a quotation from the poem is printed, describe how Vivaldi illustrates in his music the mood and meaning of the words.
7. Which of the episodes during this movement presents the greatest contrast to the ritornello? In what ways?

Minuet and Trio form

The minuet was a graceful dance, moderate in speed and with three beats to a bar, which first became fashionable at the French court in the middle of the 17th century. Baroque composers often composed minuets in pairs – the second minuet presenting some kind of contrast to the first. The two were performed in alternation, or in 'sandwich fashion':

Minuet I	Minuet II	Minuet I

Originally, whereas Minuet I was played by the whole orchestra, Minuet II was often scored for three instruments only. For this reason, the second minuet became known as the *trio* (Italian for 'three'). The custom was to omit any repeats in the first minuet when it was played again after the trio. Other dances, such as gavottes and bourrées, and sometimes pieces which were not dances at all, were similarly composed in pairs to be performed in the same way. Since all these pieces were written to the same basic plan, the name 'minuet and trio' came to describe the form itself.

The overall shape of a piece or movement in minuet and trio form is ternary:
A^1: Minuet section – ending in the tonic key;
B: Trio (Minuet II) – a contrast, usually in a new key;
A^2: Minuet section again – this time without repeats.

However, each of the main sections (both minuet and trio) is in fact a complete binary or ternary design in itself:

A^1: Minuet	B: Trio (a contrast)	A^2: Minuet (without repeats)
‖: a :‖ b(a) :‖	‖: c :‖: d(c) :‖	‖ a ‖ b(a) ‖

In the second half of the 18th century, composers included a Minuet and Trio in compositions such as symphonies, string quartets and other chamber works, and also in some sonatas. In most symphonies by Haydn and Mozart, the Minuet and Trio is placed third in the order of movements. Although the trio section is no longer for only three instruments, there is usually a noticeable change in orchestration (often featuring solos for wind instruments) and a lightness of musical texture in contrast to the fuller sound of the minuet section.

Minuet from Symphony No. 36 in C (The 'Linz')
Mozart (1756–1791)

This symphony is known as the 'Linz' because Mozart composed it during his stay at the home of Count Thun in Linz, Austria, during the autumn of 1783. On October 31, Mozart wrote to his father: 'On Tuesday November 4 I am giving a concert in the theatre here, and as I haven't a single symphony with me, I'm scribbling a new one, which must be finished in time.' The symphony was indeed ready in time and was performed by the Count's private orchestra, which consisted of oboes, bassoons, horns, trumpets, kettle drums and strings.

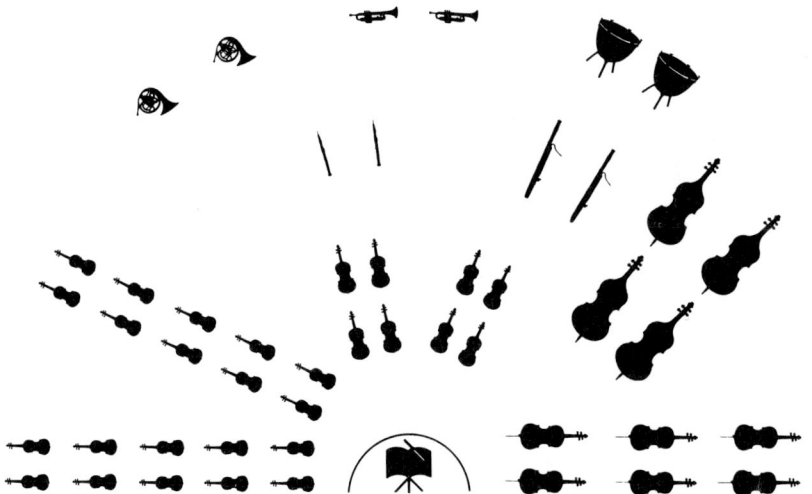

Before listening

Look through the score, on the next two pages, of this third movement of Mozart's 'Linz' Symphony. Notice especially where repeat markings occur.

As you listen

Be ready for all the repeats – but remember, repeats are *omitted* in the Minuet when it is played again after the Trio.

Follow-up

1. In which key is the Minuet?
2. Which of these types of cadence does Mozart use at bars 9–10?

   | perfect | imperfect | plagal | interrupted |

3. To which key has the music modulated by bars 17–18? How is this key related to the tonic key?
4. With what kind of cadence does the Minuet end? In which key?
5. In the Trio, which instruments are featured solo?
6. What is the meaning of: *sempre p*; *Menuetto D.C.*?
7. In which of these musical forms is the Trio structured?

   | binary form | ternary form | simple rondo form |

8. The Trio is, unusually, in the same key as the Minuet – but Mozart still makes sure that there is contrast. In what ways does the Trio contrast with the Minuet?
9. Mozart provides no tempo marking for this movement of the symphony. Which of the following best matches the speed of the music?
    Largo; *Andante*; *Allegretto*; *Presto*.
10. What is a symphony?

Scherzo and Trio

Towards the end of the 18th century, composers such as Haydn increased the pace of the minuet – often bringing a robust, outdoor flavour to what had once been a graceful courtly dance. Beethoven increased the pace still further and transformed the Minuet and Trio into the swifter, even more vigorous Scherzo and Trio (*scherzo* meaning 'a joke'), but usually keeping to the same basic plan:

Scherzo	Trio (a contrast)	Scherzo (without repeats)

Scherzo from Piano Sonata No. 2 in A major   Beethoven (1770–1827)

Beethoven's first three piano sonatas were published, as his Opus 2, in 1796. He dedicated them to his former teacher, Joseph Haydn.

Before listening

Investigate the score and discover where all repeat markings occur.

Follow-up

Listen to the music again, and discover answers to these questions:
1. The main musical idea of the Scherzo section is the opening five-note figure, rippling upwards, in the right hand. In which bars is this played by the left hand?
2. Mention some of the ways in which the Trio section presents a contrast to the Scherzo section.
3. In which bars of the Trio does Beethoven use a 'dominant pedal'?
4. The Italian word *scherzo* means 'joke' or 'jest'. Mention some of the humorous or playful touches which Beethoven includes here.

Variation form (theme and variations)

This is one of the oldest musical forms. The composer first presents a tune, called the **theme**, in a fairly straightforward way. Then he builds up the music by repeating the theme as many times as he likes, but each time *varying* it – altering, or disguising it – in one or more different ways.

| Theme | Variation 1 | Variation 2 | Variation 3 | and so on . . . |

The theme itself may be in binary or ternary form. There are countless ways in which it may be varied – really limited only by the extent of the composer's musical imagination – but the most important include:
  a) decorating it with ornaments and other extra notes;
  b) presenting it with a change of harmony, mode (major/minor), speed, rhythm, metre (number of beats to a bar), or – if the music is for orchestra or ensemble – a noticeable change of instrumentation;
  c) treating the theme, or part of it, by **imitation** – one instrumental or vocal part sets off with a snatch of tune and is immediately 'imitated' by another part copying the same musical idea (if an entire melody is strictly imitated, the result is a **canon**);
  d) treating the theme, or part of it, by **inversion** (turning it upside down), **augmentation** (stretching the notes out in longer values), or **diminution** (presenting them in shorter values).

Prélude to 'L'Arlésienne' — Bizet (1838–1875)

Bizet composed his incidental music for Alphonse Daudet's play 'L'Arlésienne' in 1872. The *Prélude*, which is played before the curtain rises, is in two parts. The first part is structured as a theme and four variations, rounded off by a coda.

Theme
For his theme, Bizet chooses the melody of an old Provençal carol called *Marcho dei Rei* (The March of the Kings). The melody is in binary form. It is presented *fortissimo* and in unison (with no harmonies, all the instruments playing the same notes):

Variation 1
The theme is now richly harmonised, and played smoothly and quietly by woodwinds (clarinet, flute, cor anglais and 2 bassoons):

Variation 2
Woodwinds and horns play the theme, against an agitated accompaniment for unison strings and snare drum. There are gradual *crescendos*, each followed by a sudden drop to *pianissimo*.

Variation 3
Slower and quieter. The theme, now in the *major* key, is played *legato* by the cellos, while 2 horns add a counter-melody. There is a contrasting, *staccato* accompaniment shared between 2 bassoons.

Variation 4

The theme is now treated in vigorous march style, and is played by the full orchestra, *fortissimo*:

Then the variations are rounded off by a coda, based on the opening bars of the theme:

Follow-up

Listen to the variations again. Which variation, do you think, provides most contrast to the others? In what ways?

Variations on
Unser dummer Pöbel (K455)   Mozart (1756–1791)

Mozart composed these variations in 1784. He borrowed the theme from an opera by the German composer, Gluck. There are ten variations in the set, of which variations 1 and 4–7 are printed here.

Before listening

Look through the score and notice where repeat signs are marked.

As you listen

Discover how, in each of these variations, Mozart varies or disguises the theme. In which variations is the theme most recognizable? In which is it most disguised?

Follow-up

1. In which of these musical forms is the theme structured?

   binary   ternary   rondo

2. In which key is the theme?
3. Which of these variations is in a minor key? Which key is it?
4. Which variation makes most use of ornaments? What kind?
5. In which variation is *imitation* featured?
6. In variation IV, how does Mozart vary the opening bars of the theme each time they appear?
7. In which variation are the theme's original harmonies most changed?
8. Listen to these variations again. Which of them do you find the most musically interesting? Why?

Fourth movement from Septet in E flat

Beethoven (1770–1827)

Beethoven's Septet, Opus 20, was first performed in Vienna in April 1800. It was an immediate success, and for many years remained Beethoven's most popular composition. The music is scored for clarinet, bassoon, horn, violin, viola, cello, and double bass.

The Septet is planned in six contrasting movements:
1. In sonata form, with slow introduction
2. Slow movement – *Adagio cantabile*
3. Minuet and Trio
4. Theme and variations
5. Scherzo, with contrasting Trio
6. Slow introduction, *Andante con moto alla marcia*, leading to *Presto* in sonata form

The theme on which Beethoven bases the fourth movement is thought to be a Rhenish folksong. It is presented by violin and clarinet in alternation. Then follow five variations on the theme, and the movement is rounded off with a coda.

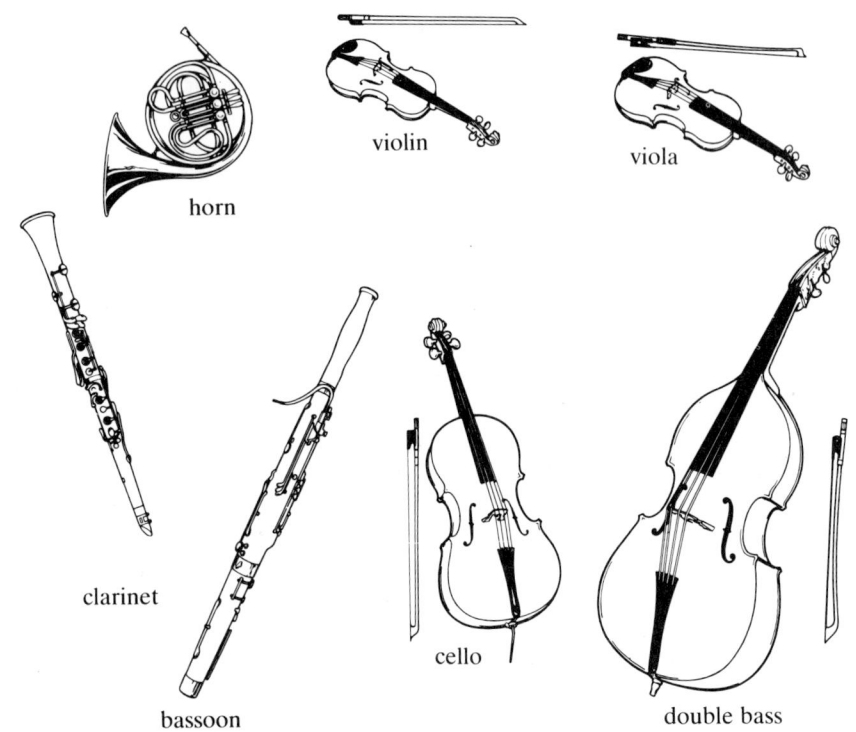

horn
violin
viola
clarinet
bassoon
cello
double bass

Follow-up

Theme (a) In which key is the theme?
(b) In which of these musical forms is the theme designed?

binary form   ternary form

Variation 1 (a) How does Beethoven vary bar 1 of the theme in this variation?
(b) How does he vary bars 3 and 4? Is it by:
imitation; *syncopation*; or *sequence*?
(c) Which two instruments play the melody in turn?

Variation 2 (a) Which two instruments share the melodic interest?
(b) What kind of note does this variation feature?

quaver   semiquaver   demisemiquaver

Variation 3 (a) Which instrument begins this variation?
(b) Which instrument follows?
(c) Name the musical device Beethoven uses to build up the music of the beginning and the end of this variation.

Variation 4 (a) How does this variation provide a sudden contrast to the previous variations?
(b) Describe the bass part at the beginning of this variation.
(c) Name an instrument which is playing *legato*.

Variation 5 (a) What does *Maggiore* indicate?
(b) Which of these instruments play the second phrase of the theme in this variation?

clarinet and horn   cello and double bass

(c) Explain the meaning of ⌐1.⌐ and ⌐2.⌐

Coda (a) At which bars in the coda does the opening phrase of the theme reappear?
(b) How does Beethoven bring humorous or comic touches into the music of the coda?

33

The Ground Bass

This is a type of variation writing, very popular during the 16th and 17th centuries, in which a theme is repeated over and over in the bass to become the *ground*, or foundation, of a composition. Above this, the composer weaves a varying texture of melody and harmonies.

In some pieces, the melody-line is structured in such a way that its phrases overlap the divisions of the ground bass, so that the seams are smoothed over and a continuous musical texture is achieved. The composer may make the uppers parts gradually more complicated, so that tension increases as the music progresses. Also, to add more variety, the theme may sometimes leave the bass and, instead, appear in an upper part of the texture.

The ground bass is also sometimes called *basso ostinato*, meaning 'obstinate bass'.

'Sound the Trumpet'   Purcell (1659–1695)

Listen to this duet from Purcell's *Come ye sons of art*, a cantata which he composed in 1694 as a birthday ode for Queen Mary. It is written for two male altos or countertenors, accompanied only by continuo. Purcell builds up the music in his favourite form – the ground bass.

Before listening

Look at the score and discover the repeating pattern of notes which forms the *ground bass* on which this music is built.

[*hautboy = oboe]

Follow-up

1. In which key does Purcell write this duet?
2. Does the ground always appear in the same key and mode?
3. Including the repeats, how many times is the ground heard during this piece?
4. Listen to the music again. Which of these words describes the way in which the two voices enter?

   | ostinato | imitation | pedal | inversion |

5. Name the instrument or instruments playing the continuo part in this music.
6. At which moments, during this music, does Purcell most vividly illustrate the mood and meaning of the words?

Finale from 'Variations on a Theme by Haydn'

Brahms (1833–1897)

Brahms composed these orchestral variations in 1873. He borrowed the theme from a suite for wind instruments by Haydn, believing that Haydn had composed the melody himself. However, it has now been discovered that Haydn had also borrowed the melody – now identified as the *St Anthony Chorale*:

Brahms writes eight variations on the theme, followed by a finale which is built upon a *ground*. The ground theme (which appears first in the bass, but is later transferred to upper parts of the musical texture) is a 'skeleton' version of bars 1–5 of the *St Anthony Chorale* theme.

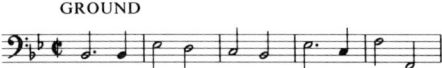

Before listening

Look through the double-stave score on the right, which traces the most important events in the music. There are 17 statements of the ground, followed by a coda in which phrases of the *St Anthony Chorale* theme reappear.

As you listen

Listen for the statements of the ground – but also try to be aware of other musical events indicated in the score.

Follow-up

1. In which key is this music written?
2. How many bars long is the *ground* on which Brahms structures this music?
3. There are 17 statements of the ground. In which of these does the ground theme appear in the treble instead of the bass?
4. Which statements of the ground are in the minor key?
5. Listen to the music again. Which statement of the ground do you find
   (a) the most vigorous?
   (b) the most expressive?
   (c) the most interesting from the point of view of musical texture and/or timbre (instrumentation)?
6. The music gradually builds to a climax – crowned, at bars 88–96, by the opening phrases of the *St Anthony Chorale* theme (see opposite). In which of the following ways does Brahms now present the theme?

   | augmentation | diminution | inversion |

7. Which bars of the *St Anthony Chorale* theme appear at bar 97 onwards?

Project 2

In each of the following five pieces, the composer builds up the music in either minuet and trio form, or some type of variation form.

1. Third movement from Clarinet Quintet in A major (K581) Mozart (1756–1791)

For the third movement of his Clarinet Quintet, Mozart writes a Minuet with *two* Trios. After each Trio, the Minuet is played again, without repeats. (Note: in some performances, the second repeat in each Trio may be omitted.)

Follow-up

1. In which of the following musical forms is the Minuet structured?

   | binary | ternary |

2. In which form is Trio I?
3. In which form is Trio II?
4. Which of the following describes the shape of the movement as a *whole*?

   | binary | ternary | rondo | variations |

5. Listen to the movement again, in sections, and briefly describe how each Trio contrasts with the Minuet. For instance, think about: key; timbre (instrumentation); rhythm and texture; style of composing and/or playing; any other points of interest.

2. *Scherzo* from Symphony No. 2 in D Beethoven (1770–1827)

Beethoven completed his Second Symphony in 1802. It is in four movements, and this Scherzo is the third movement. Beethoven scores the symphony for the usual 'Classical orchestra': 2 flutes, 2 oboes, 2 clarinets, 2 bassoons; 2 horns, 2 trumpets; 2 kettle drums; and strings.

Follow-up

1. Explain the meaning of each of these markings, found in the score:
   Allegro (♩. = 100) *cresc.* *decresc.* *fp* *sf* *Scherzo da capo*
2. In which musical form is this movement structured?
3. Listen to the Trio section again. Which instruments play the first part?
4. At which bar of the Trio are trumpets and drums first heard?
5. Which of the following is the plan of the Trio?

   ‖: A :‖: B :‖   ‖: A¹ :‖: B A² :‖   ‖: A :‖: B C :‖

6. Listen to the complete movement again. Much of the humour in this Scherzo is due to swift, violent contrasts. Note down the contrasts you hear. For example, are there contrasts (sudden changes) of:

   | dynamics | pitch | rhythm | time or metre | key |

   | tempo (speed) | timbre (instrumentation) | texture |

3. Brigg Fair
Delius (1862–1934)

In 1906 Delius heard Percy Grainger's arrangement, for solo tenor and mixed choir, of the old Lincolnshire folksong 'Brigg Fair'. Delius was so attracted by the melody that, a year later, he used it in an orchestral piece which he called *Brigg Fair: An English Rhapsody*. The score below shows the slow introduction (giving the main instruments taking part), and then the first main section of the piece in melody-line score.

Follow-up

1. Listen again to the Introduction (bars 1–19).
   (a) Describe the mood of the music.
   (b) What ingredients or qualities in the music especially help to conjure up this mood?
2. Listen again to the Theme – the folksong 'Brigg Fair'.
   (a) Which instrument plays the melody?
   (b) How are the string instruments played during the first few bars?
   (c) Which of these words describes the melody?

major	minor	chromatic	modal	atonal

3. Listen to the rest of the extract. In each of the variations, Delius makes very few changes to the melody itself. But he varies the *instrumentation*, and also the style and texture of the *accompaniment*. As you listen to each variation:
   i) note down the instrument, or instruments, playing the theme;
   ii) write a brief comment describing the accompaniment.

4. Variations on a Shaker song from the ballet 'Appalachian Spring'   Copland (born 1900)

The Shaker song on which Copland bases this brief set of variations is called 'Simple Gifts'. The melody is introduced by a clarinet:

As you listen

Discover how many variations Copland writes on his chosen theme.

Follow-up

Listen to the music again, in sections. Briefly describe how Copland varies his theme each time. Consider, for example: instrumentation; tempo (speed); accompaniment; the use of any special devices (such as imitation, ostinato); beat and/or rhythm; musical texture.

5. The Death of Falstaff   Walton (1902–1983)

This is from the incidental music Walton composed in 1943 for Laurence Oliver's film 'Henry V' (based on Shakespeare's play). Walton bases this short piece on the following *ground*:

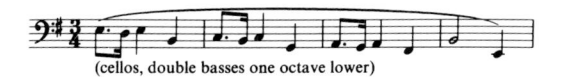

As you listen

Discover how many times the ground is stated.

Follow-up

Listen to the music again. Draw, and complete, a diagram like the one below, showing the various pitch-levels at which the ground appears.

High		
Middle		4
Low	1 2	

Da capo aria

Many arias composed between 1650 and 1750 were structured in what is known as **da capo form**; that is, in ternary form (**A¹ B A²**) but with only the first two sections of music written out. At the end of the contrasting second section (**B**) the composer wrote *da capo* (or simply *D.C.*) meaning 'from the beginning'.

Here is a more detailed plan of a da capo aria:

- **A¹**   instrumental introduction;
  first vocal solo, beginning and ending in the tonic key;
  instrumental postlude.

- **B**   second vocal solo (in a different key from the first, and often with more modulation; usually with a lighter accompaniment).

- **A²**   as **A¹** (but perhaps without the instrumental introduction).

Depending upon the style and mood of the aria, the singer, when repeating the first section, would add his or her own vocal decorations to the printed melody. And it became customary, in many operatic arias, to improvise a *cadenza* – a florid passage displaying the brilliance of the singer's technique – just before the final cadence of either **B** or **A²**.

Aria: *Dove sei* from Act I of 'Rodelinda'   Handel (1685–1759)

Handel's *opera seria* 'Rodelinda' was first performed in 1725 in London. Bertarido, King of Longobardi, has been vanquished in battle by the treacherous Grimoaldo and has fled his kingdom. He longs to be reunited with his wife, Rodelinda, to whom false news has been given that he is dead. Bertarido sings the aria *Dove sei* while standing beside his supposed tomb . . .

Handel intended the part of Bertarido to be sung by a male alto, though it is usually performed nowadays by a female singer. The aria *Dove sei* is often sung in a version with the words translated as 'Art thou troubled?' – in which case the higher-sounding instruments are given more notes to play, and bar 18 is omitted.

Aria [A] Where are you, dearest beloved?
Come to console my spirit.

[B] I am oppressed with anguish, and you alone can turn my grievous laments into joy.

Follow-up

1 In the recording you are listening to, which kind of voice sings this aria?

| soprano | mezzo-soprano | contralto | male alto |

2 Which instruments accompany the voice in section **A** of the aria?
3 In which bar does section **B** begin?
4 Which bars form the 'instrumental postlude' to the aria?
5 Listen to this da capo aria again. In what ways is music **B** different from music **A**?
6 Handel's opera 'Rodelinda' is of the type described as *opera seria*. What ingredients (both musical and dramatic) would you expect to find in an *opera seria*?

Further listening

Other da capo arias:

Handel: *Da tempeste il legno infranto* (When a ship, ravaged by storms) from the opera 'Giulio Cesare'
Sta nell' Ircana (The angry Hyrcanian tigress lurks) from the opera 'Alcina'
Rejoice greatly (soprano aria) and *Why do the nations so furiously rage together?* (bass aria) from 'Messiah'

Bach: *Grief for sin* (No. 10, alto aria) and *Break in grief* (No. 12, soprano aria) from 'St Matthew Passion'

[*In the Italian version, from bar 2; in the English version, from bar 1.]

cello

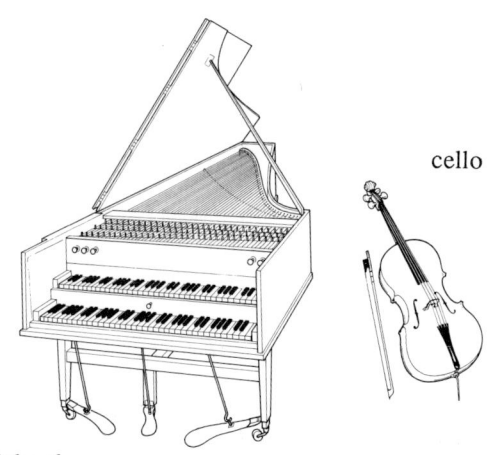

harpsichord

Lieder: strophic and through-composed

In German, the word *Lieder* simply means 'songs' (the singular is *Lied*, 'song'). But many musicians use this word with special significance – to refer only to songs by 19th-century German and Austrian Romantic composers for solo voice and piano.

The musical structure of a lied most often depends upon the poem being set. Many lieder are in **strophic** form ('verse-repeating') in which the same music is basically repeated for each verse of the poem (as in a hymn). If, for one verse, the composer makes a noticeable change (for example, changing the mode from major to minor, or vice versa) then the lied is described as being in **modified strophic** form. Some lieder are in **ternary** (three-part) form, $A^1 \, B \, A^2$, in which the middle section (B) provides some kind of musical contrast, and A^2 uses the same music as A^1. Many of the finest lieder, however, are **through-composed** (a translation of the German term **durchkomponiert**). In this kind of lied there will be little or no musical repetition. The composer allows the words to determine the structure of the music. Throughout, each line of words is set to fresh music, so that the voice-part can more faithfully match the changing moods and dramatic events in the poem.

Sometimes a composer may write a **song-cycle**. This is a set or sequence of songs, usually setting poems by a single poet, and linked together by being based on the same poetic theme – perhaps even sketching a story.

Im wunderschönen Monat Mai
(Song No. 1 from 'Dichterliebe', Opus 48)   Schumann (1810–1856)

Schumann's 'Dichterliebe' (A Poet's Love) is a song-cycle for voice and piano. It contains sixteen songs, setting poems by the German poet, Heinrich Heine. Schumann composed 'Dichterliebe' in 1840, the year he married Clara Wieck. During that year he produced more than 130 songs (he later referred to it as his 'year of song').

The song which opens the song-cycle, *Im wunderschönen Monat Mai* (In the lovely month of May), is in strophic form. There are two verses, each set to the same music. The piano sets the mood of the song, and sustains it in the interlude between the verses and in the postlude which closes the song.

Follow-up

1. Describe the mood of Schumann's music in this song. In what ways does his music bring out ideas in Heine's poem?
2. The song is strophic (two separate verses set to the same music) yet it flows smoothly from beginning to end without obvious 'stops and starts'. How does Schumann achieve this?
3. With which of these cadences does Schumann end this opening song of his song-cycle?

   | imperfect | perfect | interrupted |

   What is the musical effect of this? What do you think Schumann's reason might be for creating this effect here?

Further listening

Other lieder structured in strophic form:

Schubert: *Heidenröslein* (Rose among the heather)
Das Wandern (Wandering) and *Ungeduld* (Impatience – 'I'll carve her name on every tree') – Nos. 1 and 7 of the song-cycle 'Die Schöne Müllerin' (The fair maid of the mill)
Die Forelle (The trout) – in modified strophic form, with an important change at the beginning of verse 3

Brahms: *Der Schmied* (The blacksmith)
Wiegenlied (Lullaby, or Cradle song)

1. In the lovely month of May,
   when all the buds were opening,
   then also, in my heart,
   love began to unfold.

2. In the lovely month of May,
   when all the birds were singing,
   then I confessed to her
   my longing and desire.

Erlkönig (The Erlking)   Schubert (1797–1828)

Schubert composed his song *The Erlking* in 1815, when he was 18 years old. It is a setting of a poem by Goethe. One dark and misty night, Goethe heard the sound of galloping hooves approaching his house. Looking from his window, he glimpsed the dark figure of a horseman riding past at desperate speed, his arm cradled around a boy sitting in front of him. To Goethe it seemed as if the boy were dead. Then swiftly, the horse and its two riders were swallowed up in the mist. This strange experience gave Goethe the idea for a poem which he called *Erlkönig*; a few years later, Schubert set the poem to music.

Schubert's song is *durchkomponiert* (see page 44). Both the piano part and the voice part are fiendishly difficult. The pianist plays thundering octaves and chords in triplets throughout most of the song, striking an atmosphere of terror. The singer must change his voice to present three characters: the terrified boy, the father who is trying to comfort him, and the dreaded Erlking – the demon who haunts the forest through which they are desperately riding.

The score beginning below shows the piano introduction to the song, then continues with the voice part.

Narrator: Who rides through the night when the wind is high?
A father clasping his child rides by.
His strong arm holds him secure from harm
And wraps him closely and keeps him warm.

Father: My boy, why cover your eyes with your hands?

Boy: The Erlking, father – look where he stands!
A crown he carries, a sweeping train;

Father: My boy, it's only the mist and rain.

Erlking: Come down with me, you handsome boy,
I've many a game and many a toy;
There's flow'rs to pick and there's fine clothes to wear,
And in all my mother has you may share.

Boy: But father, oh father, you hear what he sings,
You hear him telling of all the fine things?

Father: There, there boy! There is nothing to mind,
It's only the leaves that are tossed by the wind.

Erlking: Come down, pretty boy, come down and play
For here you may do as you like all day,
And after the revels that nightly they keep,
My maidens will rock you and sing you to sleep,
My maidens will rock you and sing you to sleep.

Boy: Oh! father, oh! father, I feel so afraid,
The Erlking's maidens are there in the shade.

Father: No, no! my boy, it's only the gleam
That shines on the willows down by the stream.

Erlking: You shall be mine, I'll seize you,
And should you resist,
My strength shall not spare you,
My will shall insist.

Boy: Oh! father, dear father, he won't let me go,
Erlking is hurting me, hurting so.

Narrator: The father shuddered, he spurred on amain.
He heard beside him a low moan of pain.
He reached his home in mortal dread,
In his arms – the boy was dead.

Follow-up

1. How does Schubert create a feeling of tension in this music?
2. Which type of voice sang *The Erlking* in the recording you heard?
3. Describe how the singer changed his voice to portray each of the three characters: the father, the boy, the Erlking.
4. Listen to *The Erlking* again.
   (a) Which of the three parts (the father, the boy, or the Erlking) do you find most interesting musically?
   (b) Which of the three parts is given a style of accompaniment which is different from the others? How is it different?
5. Describe the musical and dramatic effect of the last few bars of the song (from bar 131).
6. In *The Erlking*, do you think that:
   i) the piano part is more important than the voice part,
   ii) the voice part is the most important;
   or iii) voice and piano are brought together in equal partnership?

Further listening

Other lieder which are through-composed (durchkomponiert):
Loewe: *Edward* – a dramatic setting of the Scottish ballad 'Why does your brand (sword) so drip with blood, Edward, Edward?'
Schubert: *Wohin* (Whither?) – second song from *Die Schöne Müllerin*
Brahms: *Von ewiger Liebe* (Eternal love)

Project 3

Listen to this song by Schubert; then answer the following questions.

Der Tod und das Mädchen
(Death and the maiden)

After listening

1. Is this song *strophic*, or *durchkomponiert* (through-composed)?
2. Describe any similarities and/or differences between the music of the first part (the Maiden) and that of the second part (Death).

Further exploration

Listen to part of the second movement of Schubert's String Quartet No. 14 in D minor, known as 'Death and the Maiden'. Schubert structures this slow movement as a set of variations on his song *Der Tod und das Mädchen*. The first eight bars of the theme are based on the piano introduction to the song. The last eight bars of the theme are based on the piano part of bars 30–37 of the song.

Canon and Fugue

A **canon** (from Greek, meaning 'rule') is a contrapuntal piece, or a section of a piece, which essentially relies upon *imitation*. One vocal or instrumental part leads off with a melody, and then, shortly afterwards, a second part begins the same melody. And so the 'rule' is that the second part imitates, note for note, the melody being given out by the leading part. The imitating part may follow at a distance of half a bar, one bar, two bars, or any other distance, according to the composer's choice. Other parts may also enter, successively, with the same melody.

There are several varieties of canon – depending upon the method of imitation. The second part may imitate the melody at the same pitch as the first (described as **canon at the unison**), or an octave higher or lower (**canon at the octave**), a fifth higher or lower (**canon at the fifth**), or at any other interval – again, according to the composer's choice. In a **double canon**, *two* melodies are given out simultaneously by two parts, and imitated by another two parts – two canons, on two different melodies, going on at once.

Other varieties of canon include:
(a) **canon by inversion**: the imitating part presents the melody in inversion ('turned upside down') – intervals originally rising in pitch, now fall by the same amount (and vice versa).
(b) **canon by augmentation**: the imitating part gives out the melody in longer note-values (usually doubled).
(c) **crab canon** (*canon cancrizans*) or **retrograde canon**: the imitating part gives out the melody backwards – beginning with the last note and ending with the first.
(d) **mirror canon** – this has two meanings: (1) a crab canon, or (2) a canon in which the imitating part presents the melody in inversion (upside down) *and* backwards at the same time!
(e) **infinite canon** or **perpetual canon**: in this kind of canon, as each part reaches the end of the melody it goes back to the beginning and starts all over again. A **round** (such as *Frère Jacques*) is an infinite canon at the unison.

A canon may also be described in figures. The first figure refers to the number of parts; the second indicates the number of melodies being imitated. For example, **canon 2 in 1** means a single melody, given out by one part, is imitated by one other part. In **canon 3 in 1** a single melody is imitated first by one part, then by another. **Canon 4 in 2** is the same as *double canon* (explained above).

Farandole from *'L'Arlésienne' Suite 2*   Bizet (1838–1875)

Listen to the opening of this piece. It begins with four phrases of a Provençal carol called *Marcho dei Rei* (March of the Kings) played majestically by the full orchestra in harmony. (This is the tune shown on the top stave of the score below.) Then the tune is played in canon – the first (leading) part is played by violins, oboes and clarinets; the second (imitating) part is played by violas, cellos, bassoons and horn. Notice that, in the second part, the ending of the tune is adjusted – so that the parts end up at the same time.

Follow-up

1. At what distance in time (how many beats later) does the second part imitate the first part in this canon?
2. Is the imitation: at the unison, at the octave, or at the 5th?
3. Which of the following describes this canon?

   | canon 2 in 1 | canon 3 in 1 | canon 4 in 2 |

Chorale prelude: *In dulci jubilo*   Bach (1685–1750)

This is from Bach's *Orgelbüchlein*, a collection of 46 short chorale preludes for organ, mostly composed between 1713 and 1717. The chorale melody Bach chooses here, *In dulci jubilo* (In sweet joy), is one of the oldest and best-known Christmas carols, dating from the 14th century. Bach presents the melody in canon between the top part and the pedals – though in this piece, unusually, the pedals do not play the lowest notes in the musical texture.

In dulci jubilo

(Canone doppio all' Ottava a 2 Clav. e Pedale)

J. S. Bach

Follow-up

1. (a) Look at the opening bars of this chorale prelude. At what distance (how many beats or bars later) does the second part imitate the first with the *In dulci jubilo* melody?
   (b) Is it always the *same* distance?
2. Investigate the score again. The *In dulci jubilo* melody is not the only melody being presented in canon. This is a *canon 4 in 2* (Bach's Italian subtitle means 'double canon at the octave for two manuals and pedals). In other parts of the musical texture, until bar 24, a second melody (mainly in triplets) is also heard in canon. Listen again to this chorale prelude, and try to pick out this other canon.
3. What is a 'chorale prelude'?

Further listening – other canons

Sumer is icumen in – the earliest known composition to be built up entirely in canon, composed around 1240

Haydn: Minuet from Symphony No. 44 in E minor, nicknamed the *Trauer* or 'Mourning' Symphony

Mozart: Minuet and Trio from Serenade No. 12 in C minor (K388) for 2 horns, 2 oboes, 2 clarinets and 2 bassoons. The Trio, for oboes and bassoons only, is a 'canon by inversion': oboe II presents the melody, imitated two bars later by oboe I playing the melody in inversion (upside down).

César Franck: fourth movement from Violin Sonata in A major – first the piano leads in playing the long, lyrical melody; then, a little later, the violin leads.

Fugue

A **fugue** is a contrapuntal piece, essentially based upon *imitation*. The texture is woven from separate strands of melody (usually three or four) called **parts** or **voices** (whether the fugue is vocal or instrumental). These are usually referred to as soprano, alto, tenor, bass.

A fugue is structured in three main sections, called **exposition, middle section**, and **final section**. But these sections are by no means as clearcut as those in musical forms such as ternary or rondo. In fact, many musicians do not count fugue as a musical form at all; instead, they define it as a *texture*, or *style* of composing. No two fugues are exactly alike in structural detail, but here is a brief description of the basic characteristics of a four-part fugue:

EXPOSITION   The entire fugue grows mainly from a fairly brief tune called the **subject**. The exposition begins with the subject presented in the tonic key in one voice, unaccompanied. A second voice then answers, a 5th higher or a 4th lower in the dominant key, with the same tune – but it is now referred to as the **answer** (see the diagram opposite). If it is an *exact* imitation of the subject, it is called a 'real' answer; if any intervals are at all modified, it is a 'tonal' answer. A third voice follows with the subject (tonic), and a fourth voice replies with the answer (dominant). The voices may enter in any order according to the composer's choice.

Each voice, after stating subject or answer, continues with another tune in counterpoint. If each voice presents the *same* tune, it is called the **counter-subject**. However, should a voice continue with a tune which does not recur regularly, it is then called a **free part**.

After the fourth voice has completed the answer, the first voice may be given an 'extra' entry of the subject – called a **redundant entry** – so that the fourth voice also has a chance of stating the counter-subject. The counter-subject must be written in 'invertible counterpoint', since it must sound equally well above or below either subject or answer.

Sometimes a composer delays a succeeding entry of subject or answer for a moment or so. The intervening linking music, however brief, is called a **codetta** (a quite different meaning from codetta in sonata form).

MIDDLE SECTION   In this section entries of the subject, called **middle entries**, occur in related keys (usually avoiding the tonic key). These middle entries may appear singly, or in groups – as subject and answer. Other passages of music occur called **episodes**. These serve as modulating links, and also offer relief from entries of the subject. However, whereas in forms such as ternary and rondo an episode is a complete contrast, an episode in fugue is frequently based on a fragment taken from either the subject or the counter-subject.

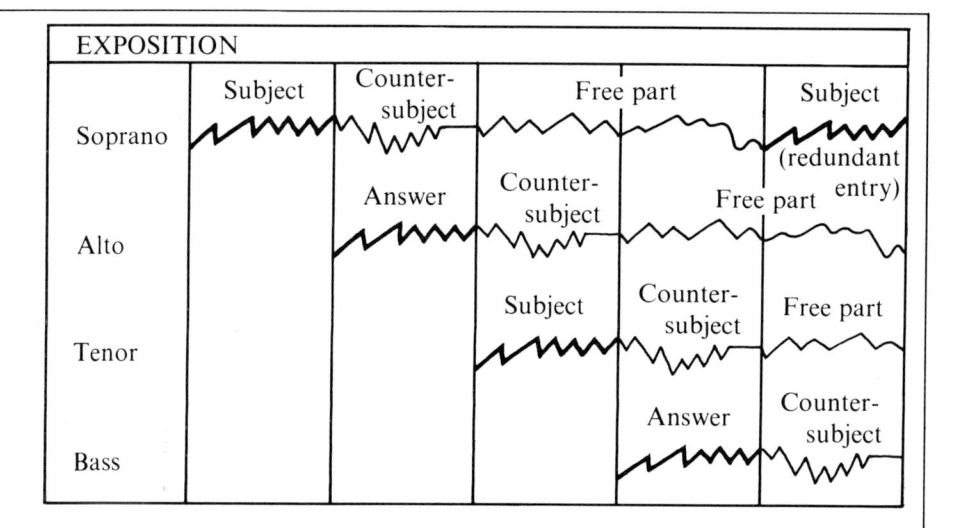

EXPOSITION					
Soprano	Subject	Counter-subject		Free part	Subject
Alto		Answer	Counter-subject		Free part (redundant entry)
Tenor			Subject	Counter-subject	Free part
Bass				Answer	Counter-subject

FINAL SECTION   This begins when the subject returns in the tonic key once more. It may occur in one voice only, or several in turn. Any music after the end of the last complete entry is called the **coda**. (In some fugues, the last entry occurs *in* the coda.)

During the middle and/or the final section, the music may be made more exciting by use of certain devices – either singly, or in combination:
a) **pedal** (short for *pedal point*): a note, usually the dominant or the tonic, sustained or repeated in the bass beneath changing harmonies. In an *inverted pedal*, the note is sounded in the highest part; in an *internal pedal*, in an inner part.
b) **inversion**: the subject is 'turned upside down' – intervals originally rising in pitch, now fall by the same amount (and vice versa).
c) **augmentation**: the notes stretched out in longer values (usually double).
d) **diminution**: the notes presented in shorter values (usually half).
e) **stretto** (Italian, 'squeezed together'): an overlapping of entries of subject and answer. In a *close stretto* the overlapping occurs very swiftly; in a *stretto maestrale* (masterly stretto) all voices take part, each presenting subject or answer complete and unmodified.

Fugue means 'flight' – giving an idea of the voices fleeing away, or chasing each other, as they enter with subject or answer.

Fugue in C minor for 3 voices,
from Book 1 of 'The Well-tempered Clavier' (or 'The 48') Bach (1685–1750)

Follow-up

1. Name the three 'voices' in the order in which they enter.
2. The answer is 'tonal'. Which note or notes would need altering to make the answer 'real'?
3. Which of these devices does Bach use at the end of the fugue?

   | inversion | augmentation | tonic pedal | dominant pedal |

4. With what kind of cadence does Bach end the fugue?

Further investigation

Examine the music, then listen to the fugue again, and discover whether or not Bach includes a *counter-subject*.

Further exploration

If you can, listen to this fugue recorded by the Swingle Singers, and compare their version with Bach's original keyboard version. In what ways are the two versions different? How are they similar?

First two movements from Concerto Grosso in G minor, Opus 6 No. 6   Handel (1685–1759)

Each of Handel's twelve *Concerti Grossi* Opus 6, composed in 1739, is for a concertino group of 2 violins and cello, ripieno strings, and continuo. (Handel later added 2 oboes to the ripieno group in Concertos 1, 2, 5 and 6.) The sixth concerto is in five movements. The first has the rhythm of a sarabande. The quick second movement is a fugue.

Before listening

Look through the score to see how the various instrumental parts are arranged on the page. In the first movement, the two solo violin parts are placed above the ripieno violins. The solo cello and ripieno cellos share the same stave, and the lowest stave is for double bass(es) and continuo. In the second movement, the concertino group doubles (plays the same notes as) the ripieno group.

Solo
Tutti
Solo
Tutti
Allegro, ma non troppo
Violino I
conc. e rip.
Violino II
Viola
Tutti Bassi
(codetta)
Violonc. solo
Tutti
Episode

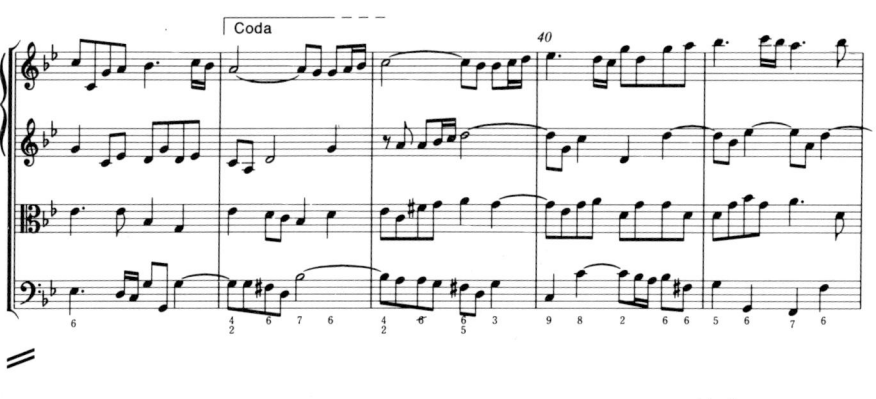

Follow-up

First movement:
1. What is the meaning of each of these terms, found in the score?
   concertino ripieno solo tutti
2. Explain the purpose of the figures printed below the bass-line.
3. In the recording you heard, which instrument or instruments played the *continuo* part?
4. Mention the main musical contrasts you hear in this first movement.
5. Describe the effect of the final bars.

Second movement:
6. In which key is this movement?
7. Name the instruments which enter, in turn, with subject and answer during the exposition of this fugue.
8. In which key are the two entries of the answer?
9. Is the answer 'tonal' or 'real'?
10. At which bar does the middle section of the fugue begin?
11. At which bar does the final section begin? In which key is the final entry of the fugue subject?
12. Describe the main differences in timbre and texture between these two movements. What is the difference in mood?

Project 4

The next two scores are two items, a recitative and a chorus, from Part II of Handel's *Messiah*. In a complete performance of *Messiah*, they follow the three choruses: 'Surely He has borne our griefs', 'And with His stripes we are healed', and 'All we like sheep have gone astray'.

As you listen

During the recitative notice, especially, Handel's accompaniment to the voice-part.

The chorus which follows is a choral fugue, based on the subject introduced in bars 1–5 (opposite). Listen for this rhythmic melody throughout the fugue. And, according to pitch, spot which voice-part (soprano, alto, tenor, or bass) is entering with subject or answer.

After listening

1. Which type of voice sings the recitative?

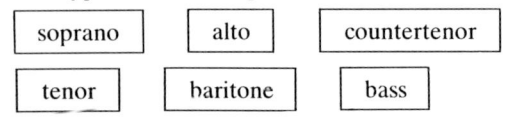

    | soprano | alto | countertenor |

    | tenor | baritone | bass |

2. Name the instruments which accompany the voice.
3. Which of these terms describes this particular style of recitative?

    | secco | stromentato |

4. At certain points in the accompaniment, Handel reflects events taking place by making his music pictorial, or illustrative. Where does he do this, and how?
5. In which key is the fugue 'He trusted in God'?
6. In which order do the voice-parts enter with subject and answer during the exposition of the fugue?
7. Is the answer 'tonal', or 'real'?
8. In this fugue there are four *episodes*, and in each one, Handel uses the same phrase of words over and over again.
    (a) In which bar does the first episode begin?
    (b) Which words are repeated, again and again?
    (c) Which of these devices does the music strongly feature?

    | ostinato | imitation | inversion | sequence |

9. Listen to the fugue again, and spot the remaining episodes.

No. 27 Recitative: All they that see Him

Psalm XXII, v.7

No. 28 Chorus: *He trusted in God*

Psalm XXII, v.8

[MIDDLE SECTION]

30
He trust - ed in God that he would de - li - ver him,
- light in him, let him de - li - ver him, if
trust - ed in God, he trust - ed in God, let him de - li - ver him, if
35
let him de - li - ver him, if he de - light in
- li - ver him, let him de - li - ver him, if he de -
He trust - ed in God that he
let him de - li - ver him,
let him de - li - ver him, if he de-light in him,
he de-light in him, if he de-light in him, let him de -
he de - light in him, if he de-light in him, let him de - li - ver him.
let him de - li - ver him,
8ves.
him, if he de - light in him, let him de - li - ver him,
- light in him, let him de -
would de - li - ver him, let him de - li - ver him,
let him de - li - ver him.

40
if he de-light in him, let him de - li - ver him,
- li - ver him, if he de - light in him. He trust - ed in God, let him de -
if he de-light in him, let him de - li - ver him. He trust - ed in God, let him de -
He trust - ed in God that he
8ves.
- li - ver him, let him de - li - ver him, let him de - li - ver him,
him, let him de - li - ver him, if he de -
him, let him de - li - ver him,
him, let him de - li - ver him,
45
let him de -
- li - ver him, if he de - light in
- li - ver him, if he de - light in
would de - li - ver him, let him de - li - ver him, if he de-light in
[FINAL SECTION]
50
He trust - ed in God that he would de -
- light in him. He trust - ed in God, let him de - li - ver
if he de - light in him, if he de - light,
if he de-light in him, if he de - light
8ves.

60
- li - ver him, let him de - li - ver him, if he de - light in him,
him, if he de - light in him, let him de - li - ver him, let him de -
if he de - light in him,
in him, if he de - light in him, let him de - li - ver him.
- light in him, let him de - li - ver him,
in him, let him de - li - ver him,
in him, let him, let him de - li - ver him,
God that he would de - li - ver him, let him, let him, de - li - ver him,
60
55
if he de - light in him, if he de -
- li - ver him, if he de - light
let him de - li - ver him, if he de-light in him, if he de - light
He trust - ed in
55
8ves.
Adagio
if he de - light in him.
if he de - light in him.
if he de - light in him.
if he de - light in him.
Adagio

Sonata form

This is one of the most important of all musical forms. The name is rather misleading. 'Sonata form' does not refer to the structure of a complete work, but to a special form used to build up a single movement of a work. Also, this form is used in other works besides sonatas, such as symphonies and string quartets. In works like these, the first movement is almost always in sonata form, and sometimes one or more of the other movements as well. Overtures, too, are often built up in sonata form.

Sonata form grew, in several stages, from *binary* (two-part) form, but in outline it is *ternary* (three-part) since the overall structure divides into three main sections called **exposition**, **development**, and **recapitulation**. There may be an introduction (usually in a slow tempo) before the actual sonata form begins.

1 Exposition In this section the composer 'exposes', or presents, his musical material. The main ideas are called **subjects** (in the sense of 'subjects for later discussion'). There are two subjects – and each may consist of a *group* of ideas, rather than a single melody. The two subjects are contrasted in key, and usually also in mood or character.

The **first subject** is presented in the tonic key. Then follows the **bridge passage**, which modulates (changes key) and leads to the **second subject** in a new, but usually related, key – often the dominant if the tonic is major, or the dominant or the relative major if the tonic is minor. The second subject is usually more melodious, less vigorous than the first subject. The final part of the second subject is called the *codetta* – a 'small coda' or closing section, rounding off the exposition.

Composers sometimes mark the end of the exposition with repeat signs, so the whole of this section may be played again.

2 Development In this section the composer explores new keys (usually avoiding the tonic key) while discussing and developing any of the musical ideas so far presented. (Entirely new ideas, called 'episodic' material, may also be introduced).

Any aspect of the musical material – melodic, rhythmic or harmonic – may be brought under musical discussion or development. Themes may be broken down into fragments, and these fragments then built up in new ways. Fragments of different ideas may be combined – or set in opposition, one against another. A powerful feeling of tension and dramatic conflict may be built up, emphasized by modulations through contrasting keys, and reaching a climax when the music purposefully makes for 'home' – the tonic key – and the beginning of the recapitulation section.

3 Recapitulation The composer now 'recapitulates', or states in a slightly different form, the music of the exposition section. The first subject returns in the tonic key, as before. But the bridge passage is altered so that the second subject now *also* returns in the tonic key. The sonata form is usually rounded off by a **coda**.

(The above description, and the diagram below, give only the basic plan of sonata form. A composer may make some kind of alteration, or add further interesting details, to achieve a certain musical effect.)

Sonata form							
EXPOSITION (presentation)			**DEVELOPMENT (discussion)**	**RECAPITULATION (restatement)**			**CODA**
		SECOND SUBJECT (in a new, but related key)	Exploring new keys while discussing and developing, combining and opposing, ideas presented in the exposition				
FIRST SUBJECT (in the tonic key)	BRIDGE PASSAGE (changing key)			FIRST SUBJECT (in tonic key as before)	BRIDGE PASSAGE altered to lead to:	SECOND SUBJECT (now *also* in the tonic key)	to round off

Overture – *The Hebrides (Fingal's Cave)* Mendelssohn (1809–1847)

Fingal's cave, on the island of Staffa in the Hebrides, can only be approached from the sea. At high tide the waves crash into the cave, while seabirds wheel and skim, uttering sharp piercing cries. Mendelssohn visited Fingal's cave during his stay in Scotland in 1829. It proved to be a rough journey – and Mendelssohn was a poor sailor. But the wild beauty of the scene inspired him to compose his overture *The Hebrides*, which he subtitled *Fingal's Cave*.

This is a concert overture and the music is programmatic, or descriptive. Mendelssohn structures the music in sonata form, and rounds off the overture with a quite lengthy coda.

Before listening

Look through the score to see how the added brackets and labels point out the basic plan of the sonata form, matching the diagram shown opposite.

64

Follow-up

1. *The Hebrides* is a programmatic concert overture. What is a 'concert overture'?
2. Mention two or three other concert overtures you have heard. For each one, give the name of the composer.
3. (a) In which particular part of *The Hebrides* do you find Mendelssohn's music most programmatic (or descriptive)?
   (b) What images or ideas does the music conjure up in your mind at this point?
   (c) Explain in detail *how* Mendelssohn suggests these images or ideas in his music.

Further investigation

1. Compare the two appearances of the second subject, in the exposition and in the recapitulation. What changes does Mendelssohn make to the second subject when it reappears in the recapitulation?
2. Read again the explanation of the development section in sonata form on page 62. Then listen again to the development section of Mendelssohn's *The Hebrides*.
   (a) Which themes or ideas do you recognize from the exposition?
   (b) How does Mendelssohn develop or change these previously heard themes and ideas?
3. Does the *coda* consist of entirely new musical ideas – or do any ideas heard previously during the overture now reappear?

Abridged sonata form

As the name implies, this is a shortened version of sonata form. If you compare the diagram below with the one on page 62, you will see that abridged sonata form is in fact sonata form without a development section. Instead, after the exposition, a **link** leads back to the tonic key and the recapitulation. This link may be a few bars long, or just a single chord – a dominant 7th chord leading straight into the recapitulation section in the tonic key.

Because of its compactness, abridged sonata form has been used for operatic overtures, and also for slow movements of compositions such as sonatas, symphonies and chamber works where, due to the leisurely speed of the music, a full sonata form might take too long to unfold.

Abridged sonata form

EXPOSITION (presentation)			LINK	RECAPITULATION (restatement)			CODA
FIRST SUBJECT (in the tonic key)	BRIDGE PASSAGE (changing key)	SECOND SUBJECT (in a new, but related key)	joining the exposition to the recapitulation	FIRST SUBJECT (in tonic key as before)	BRIDGE PASSAGE altered to lead to:	SECOND SUBJECT (now *also* in the tonic key)	to round off

Overture to
La Gazza Ladra

Rossini (1792–1868)

Rossini composed his opera *La Gazza Ladra* (The Thievish Magpie) for La Scala, Milan, and it was first performed in that famous opera house in 1817. A servant girl, suspected of stealing a silver spoon, is sentenced to death, but her innocence is proved when the spoon is discovered in the nest of a thievish magpie.

The music of the overture to the opera is characteristic of Rossini's style: a handful of good tunes, brilliantly and wittily orchestrated, and presented with elegance, sparkle and good humour.

Before listening

Investigate the score beginning on the right. Rossini begins his overture with a quite lengthy introduction, marked 'majestic, martial'. (In some performances, the first of the snare drum rolls may be played *forte* rather than *piano*; and bars 32–41 may be omitted.) Rossini structures the main part of the overture in abridged sonata form, with a 23-bar link joining the exposition to the recapitulation. Parts two and three of the second subject are a typical, exciting 'Rossini *crescendo*' gradually building up from *p sotto voce* to *fortissimo*.

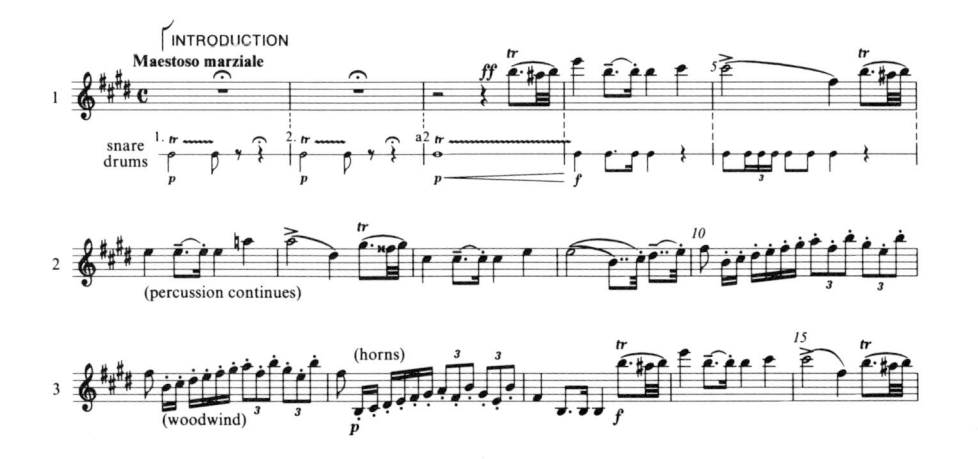

[tonic major]
cresc.
cresc.
Bridge passage
(lower strings, bassoons, bass trombone)
G.P.
p sotto voce
(bassoons, horns, trombone)
Second subject, part one [in the relative major]
(oboe)
(violins, flute)
(piccolo, clarinet, bassoon)
(Second subject, part one, repeated)
(oboe, horn, cellos)
(violins, flute)
(piccolo, clarinet, bassoon)
Second subject, part two
(horns)
(+ clarinets)
p sotto voce
snare drums

(+ snare drums)
cresc. poco a poco
poco a poco cresc.
Second subject, part three – codetta
f e sempre cresc.
LINK (at first, based on idea from bridge passage)
ff
(lower strings, bassoons, bass trombone)
pp
RECAPITULATION: First subject [in the tonic key]
p
ff
Bridge passage
G.P.
p
Second subject, part one [in the tonic major]
p
(clarinet)
(violins, flute)
(piccolo, oboe, clarinet)
(Second subject, part one, repeated)
(clarinet, horn, cellos)
(violins, flute)
(piccolo, oboe, clarinet)

Follow-up

1. Listen to the music again. Which other percussion instruments, besides snare drums, are heard during the introduction?
2. Parts two and three of the second subject are a 'Rossini *crescendo*'.
   (a) During part two, how many times is the tune played?
   (b) Describe how Rossini builds up the *crescendo*.
   (c) Which bar marks the actual climax?
3. Describe any touches of humour you notice in this overture.
4. What do you like or dislike about this piece of music?

Further investigation

When the music of the exposition reappears in the recapitulation, what is mainly different about the music of:
   (a) the first subject;
   (b) the bridge passage;
   (c) the second subject?

Sonata-rondo form

As its name suggests, sonata-rondo form combines certain ingredients of sonata form (explained on page 62) and simple rondo form (see page 12).

The basic plan of a sonata-rondo, which is symmetrical in structure, may be shown simply as **A B A C A B A**.

Like simple rondo form, sonata rondo depends upon a recurring main theme (**A**) which appears at least three times. But both this theme and the second theme (**B**), which occurs twice, are called **subjects** since they may be used for development (as 'subjects for discussion') during the central section (**C**).

Like sonata form, sonata-rondo has two subjects (the second subject returning, during the recapitulation section, in the tonic key), and the total sonata-rondo structure divides into three main sections.

However, the exposition and the recapitulation both end with a return of the principal subject (the rondo theme) or at least some reference to it. And the central section of a sonata-rondo may consist of development of previous material, or an episode introducing completely new material, or a combination of both.

There is usually a bridge passage, as in sonata form, connecting the principal subject to the second subject. At other points, a link may be used to join sections smoothly together.

Sonata-rondo form is frequently used to build up the final movement of instrumental compositions such as sonatas, symphonies, concertos, string quartets and other chamber works.

Sonata-rondo form

EXPOSITION		CENTRAL SECTION		RECAPITULATION	
A^1	Principal subject (the recurring rondo theme) in the tonic key	C	Very often an *episode* (introducing new material) in another related key; or a *development* of any previous material; or, occasionally, a combination of both	A^3	Principal subject (rondo theme) in the tonic key
	Bridge passage, changing key and leading to:				Bridge passage, now altered to lead to:
B	Second subject (usually in the dominant or the relative major)			B	Second subject – now *also* in the tonic key
A^2	Principal subject (rondo theme) in the tonic key			A^4	Principal subject (rondo theme), perhaps shortened, *and/or* a **coda** making some reference to the principal subject

Third movement from Violin Concerto in D major, Opus 61
Beethoven (1770–1827)

Beethoven's Violin Concerto, which he composed in 1806, is in three movements. The lively and humorous third movement (which follows the slow movement without a break) is built up in sonata-rondo form.

Before listening

Look through the score to see how the added brackets and labels, indicating the plan of the sonata-rondo, compare with the diagram on page 71. In this particular sonata-rondo, the central section (**C**) is an *episode* introducing a completely new melody.

As this is a concerto movement, Beethoven indicates that the soloist should play (improvise) a *cadenza* during the recapitulation section. This cadenza leads straight into A^4 – which in this sonata-rondo is a coda, mainly based on the principal subject (the recurring rondo theme).

A²: Principal subject [in the tonic key]
sul G
delicatamente
ten.
(solo violin)
dim.
CENTRAL SECTION
C: Episode [in G minor]
dolce
(above pizzicato bass)
cresc.
RECAPITULATION
A³: Principal subject [in the tonic key]

Bridge passage
dim.
pizz.
arco
B: Second subject
cresc.
(cellos)
(1st violins)
(flute)
(oboe)
(cellos, basses)
(bassoon)
(clarinet)
(solo violin)
Solo
Cadenza
A4: Coda (based on the principal subject)
(cellos, basses)
più p
(1st violins)
sempre più p
(+ 2nd violins)
sempre p
sempre pp

Follow-up

Listen to this movement again, in sections, and discover answers to these questions.

1. (a) During the first section (**A¹**) the tune is presented three times. How is it different each time?
   (b) Describe the mood presented by this first section.
2. In which key does the second subject (**B**) begin? In which key is the music at bars 62–64?
3. When the principal subject (the rondo theme) returns in **A²**, is the music the same as at first, or is it changed?

4. (a) The central section (**C**) is an episode introducing a new melody. Which instrument shares this melody with the solo violin?
   (b) What musical contrasts do you hear presented by the music of the central section, compared with the music of the exposition?

5. When the principal subject returns in **A³**, is it the same as at first, or is it changed?
6. In which key does the second subject (**B**) return, in the recapitulation?
7. Does the **cadenza** include themes or ideas heard earlier in the movement, or does it consist of new ideas?

8. (a) The **coda** (**A⁴**) is quite lengthy. The rondo theme first appears, bar 293, in a key which is surprisingly remote from the tonic key. Which key is it?
   (b) When the rondo theme eventually appears in the tonic key, which instruments play it 'in dialogue'?
   (c) In which bars of the coda does Beethoven use syncopation?
   (d) Mention other ways in which Beethoven builds up tension during the coda.
   (e) Describe the effect of the final bars of the coda.

9. Explain the meaning of: *concerto*; *cadenza*; *coda*.

Project 5

In each of the next three pieces, the composer designs and builds up the music in a special way – still, however, using the two basic ingredients of repetition and contrast to make sure that the finished work has shape and continuity, proportion and balance.

1. Jesu, Joy of Man's Desiring

Bach (1685–1750)

This well-known piece is Bach's arrangement for choir and orchestra of a chorale composed in 1641 by Johann Schopp. It forms the sixth and final movement of Bach's Cantata No. 147, composed in 1723.

Je - su, joy of man's de - sir - ing,
Ho - ly wis - dom, Love most bright.
Drawn by Thee, our souls as - pir - ing,
Soar to un - cre - a - ted light.
Word of God our flesh that fa - shioned,
With the fire of life im - pas - sioned.
Stri - ving still to truth un - known.
Soar - ing, dy - ing, round Thy throne.

Follow-up

1. Which type of instrument is most important in the accompaniment?
2. Bach presents the chorale melody in sections – so that the voices do not sing continually. How does he ensure that there is still a continuous, smooth flow of music from beginning to end?
3. What is a *chorale*?

2. Zadok the Priest — Handel (1685–1759)

Handel composed this anthem for the coronation of George II in 1727; it has been sung at each British coronation ever since. First there is an orchestral introduction. Then Handel builds up the music in clear-cut sections which, in style and mood, bring out the meaning of the text. Bars 1–40 are printed here in vocal score – showing all the voice-parts but with the orchestral parts reduced to a two-stave arrangement; the remainder is given in melody-line score only.

25
Na - than the pro - phet an - oint - ed
9
10
Sol - o - mon King.
ten.
30
Allegro
Soprano I/II
Alto I
Alto II
11 Tenor
Bass I/II
And all the peo - ple re - joic'd, re -
35
f
mf
12
- joic'd, re - joic'd, and all the peo - ple re -
40
13
joic'd, re - joic'd, re - joic'd, re -
45
più f

Follow-up

1. The anthem begins with an orchestral introduction. Mention any interesting points about the music of this introduction, leading to the entry of the voices.
2. Handel structures the anthem in clear-cut sections. How many sections are there?
3. One of the sections begins at bar 31. How is the accompaniment different from that of the previous section?
4. Listen to the anthem again. Which instruments does Handel include in his orchestra?
5. Is this a 'full anthem', or a 'verse anthem'?

3. On Hearing the First Cuckoo in Spring
Delius (1862–1934)

This tone poem, which Delius composed in 1912, is the first of his 'Two Pieces for Small Orchestra' (the second being *Summer Night on the River*). In this tone poem, Delius presents a musical description of the freshness and beauty of the countryside awakening in spring.

Delius bases *On Hearing the First Cuckoo in Spring* upon a Norwegian folk-song called 'I Ola-Dalom, i Ola-Kjönn' (In Ola valley, in Ola lake). The melody is in four phrases, A B C D:

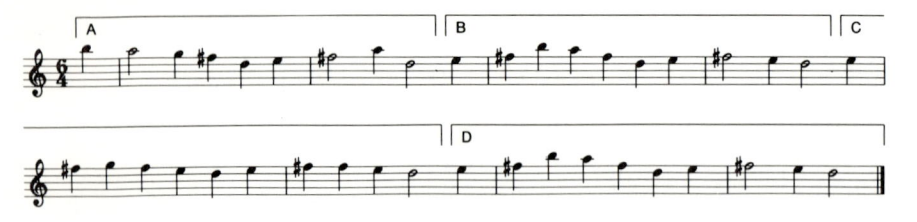

Delius brings in phrases of this melody at various pitches. And he structures the tone poem by gently weaving music of his own between and around the phrases of the folk-song. (His two main ideas occur at bars 4–9 and 10–11.)

Delius scores *On Hearing the First Cuckoo in Spring* for flute, oboe, 2 clarinets, 2 bassoons, 2 horns, and strings.

Follow-up

1. How many groups of cuckoo-calls are there during this tone poem?
2. Which instrument plays the cuckoo-calls?
3. Delius first introduces the Norwegian folk-song at the end of bar 18 – but he quotes the phrases in this pattern: A A C D D. In which bars does the folk-song appear in full, with the phrases played according to its original pattern, A B C D?
4. Describe the mood Delius conjures up in this tone poem.
5. What is a tone poem?